Million-Year Elegies

Ada Hoffmann

Remember your monsters.

A. Hoffmann

Copyright © 2021 Ada Hoffmann

All rights reserved.

ISBN: 979-8-5678-2529-7

"Hallucigenia" first appeared, as "Million-Year Elegies: Hallucigenia," in Liminality Magazine, Issue #8 (June 2016).

"Edmontonia" first appeared, as "Million-Year Elegies: Edmontonia," in Mythic Delirium 3.1 (July 2016).

"Tyrannosaurus" first appeared, as "Million-Year Elegies: Tyrannosaurus," in Uncanny Magazine, Issue 12 (September 2016).

"Oviraptor" first appeared, as "Million-Year Elegies: Oviraptor," in Strange Horizons, September 14, 2016.

"Archaeopteryx" first appeared, as "Million-Year Elegies: Archaeopteryx," in Asimov's, December 2016.

Cover design & illustration © Kelsey Liggett -
http://www.kelseyliggettillustration.com/

For Salie,
who survived

CONTENTS

	Prologue: The Late Heavy Bombardment	Pg 1
1	The Age of Monsters	Pg 3
2	The Age of Reptiles	Pg 19
3	The Age of Mammals	Pg 49
	Epilogue: Memento Mori	Pg 65

PROLOGUE:
THE LATE HEAVY BOMBARDMENT

When the stars aligned, they came for us.
The massive bones of other worlds
shook free into our path.
The baby seas, the nascent air: swept out.
The earth bucked and shuddered, beaten
by these cosmic fists, until nothing was left
but the earth's blood burning, a red magma sea
and a sky of smoke.

Listen. Listen. We were already alive.

There were those of us, single-celled and small as we were,
who found purchase on rock islands. We clustered
hanging on by our membranes. We were young.
We saw no sunlight. We learned to breathe boiling,
drink acid. You would have called it hell,
but we lived, in the cracks in those rocks.
We did not know what we waited for.

This was at dawn.
We were not flesh and bone. We knew nothing
but that we wanted to live. Eat. Grow.
To bear with our bodies yet more of us
who would live. To see-this, above all-
to see what happened next.

We lived. It took more time than you have ever dreamed.
The earth cooled, and water ran down from the sky.
Tides lapped at hardened stone, drawn by a scarred young moon.
There was soil. There were stars. Our children grew.

Listen. This world is a breakable bone,
a fragile cage in a sea of ice and flame,
and wondrous creatures cling to its edges.
This world has burned and ended, burned and ended

more times than you know, and never yet a time
worse than ours. Not yet.

We cling to the cracks in our rocks, still afraid.
We see more than you know. We look
at our children. We look at the stars.
We look at the stars.

1. THE AGE OF MONSTERS

ADA HOFFMANN

FRANCEVILLIAN BIOTA

The earth breathed in.
The earth breathed out.

We were small, soft cells
beneath a placid lake.
We grew in mats,
each lying cuddled to the next.
The world had cooled long enough ago
that cool air and comfortable waves
seemed a birthright.

The algae did not mean offense.
They were like us: small blue-green
innocent things. Sunlight sank into them.
But what came out: air that blistered,
air that burned.

We who had not known fear
committed the first panicked sin:
we ate. Dove on those algae
and tore membrane from plasm.
We sucked up the small, crushed them
in a vacuole gut, desperate for the energy
that would give us breath in this new,
blue-burning sky.

Ten million years of panic
and ten trillion victims later,
we no longer blistered.
Something stayed alive
in those vacuoles. Taking the flame
not as poison-as fuel.

We were so much bigger now.
We moved so fast. We drew together
in mountainous chorusing forms,

breathed the world in,
breathed the world out.

CLOUDINA

It felt like the end of the world, the first time.
The slow sharp grinding at my bones. After,
a hole, as though
I'd been sucked through the gap in my own shell.

We were the first, my sisters and I,
to wrap the bones of the world around us
as a shield. We were not the only ones
who took up heavy, slicing things
to arms.

The second time, the stabbing
felt like victory. It should not have,
but I rocked against those questing claws
knowing nothing ever bothers to attack
what is already dead. I am still here,

shifting in my shells. I have plans.
There will be a thousand of me
made from the blind-clawed grabbings of you,
and with all our perforations, we remain.

HALLUCIGENIA

There is a man in spectacles in Cambridge
staring at you, tracing the curled-over outline
of your long-dead self. It is he
who names you, *disconnected hallucination,*
unable to accept your shape.
      He is an expert
in your time: a time of shifting
and changing, of body plans found and discarded
as life slips the cage of single cells,
looks left and right, grins at its freedom,
gets out the brightest biomolecular Lego bricks
and plays. This man accepts an invisible God.
Yet he cannot quite believe
what he sees with his eyes: this shape
lacking head or tail, the sheer spinesplotchy
patched-together matter-of-factness of you.
      It is no matter
to you, who play hopscotch and tug-of-war
with five-eyed hose-nosers and pineapple-mouthed shrimp.
An eye, however bulging or beady or shrewd,
is only a toy for finding light. It does you no harm
if it cannot stop staring. Nor if it names you
and baptizes you in its too-tight taxonomy,
still doubting, even through the thick glass
of five hundred million years, that you
were ever real.

SHANKOUCLAVA

They may have told you: grow a spine.
This creature did, and found
that a spine was not to its liking.

Minnowlike, it swam thrashing,
trembling side to side.
The spine, a whippy core
within oneself, allows this.
It darted into crevices,
quick and fearful,
unable to eat. You understand,
this was only its larval form.

You too may find one day that you wish
to attach yourself somewhere,
to stop moving. To catch your breath
and let the waves fill you for once,
in place of your own old hardness.

TRILOBITA

The little bugs, the ancient seas,
more multitudes than can be sung.
In all the oldest shales, one sees
these little bugs. The ancient seas
that burst with life, but favored these,
their simple, sturdy forms among
the little bugs. The ancient sea's
more multitudes than can be sung.

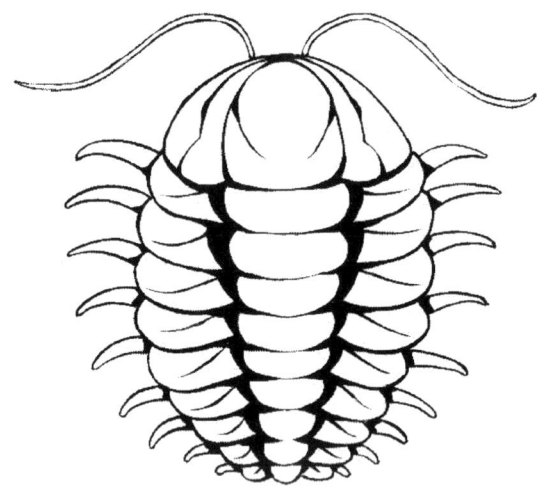

EUTHYCARCINUS

You tested the air. It was becoming routine.
One antenna rose to breach the surface tension.
Then your face, the mandibles, the eyes.
You reared on seven irregular hind legs.
The beach lay before you: bare, warm dunes,
piled in layers up and up. Beyond them, stone.
And hiding in between the grains of sand,
a thin green film, your target.
Well worth the journey,
if you could hold your breath.

Behind you, the richer lives
of weed and worm and wave went on.
Shrimp gnawed on trilobites. You scuttled forward,
raised your gills to the air, and climbed.

SHIMENOLEPIS

The jaw--fearsome lever of teeth,
knife-edged crunch, poised to crush you
as you're swallowed-

I used it to guide water through my gills.

That was all it was at first.
My kind's heads were strung
with delicate arches, softly expanding.
Only a little movement, like the ribs
of your kind, in and out.
Then more. And more.

Hungry for the breath of life.
Hungry to live. Hungry for safety,
in this skin of mine that turned
from shimmering scale to stone.
Angry. Armored. Hungry.
Pumping the water harder. Guzzling.
Until little creatures like you
fell into me as well, and more,
and more.

Food is like breath, after all.
Do you blame me? Think fast.

TIKTAALIK

As it turns out, the hand came before the foot:
a club-fin, barely fingered. Your heavy shoulder
pushed you into clearer water,
to snap at your struggling cousins
on the draggy seaweed floor.
Then higher yet: into the shallows
to gasp a breath of sharp-sweet air
when the pond around you thickened and stank.
Strange, seeking life in this thin nothing
you had so long ignored. Plants and insects
made this journey long before you, traveling lightly
where the wind and rain carried. But you:
you weren't even trying. Until the day
when the thick water hardened to mud for good,
and you dragged yourself across it
with your strong shoulders, thinking,
maybe this is not so bad: maybe here, too,
in the cold dry sky, a fish could live its life.

CYSTOIDEA

Why should we have gone to the land?
Plants were sickly dwarves up there.
We were not plants, but we lived like them,
still and happy where we stood.

We loved the sun from a distance,
rooted under clear water,
reached up to the rippling light.
Until the water churned and darkened,
all of us choking together.

Some distant cousin leered pityingly down.
Cousins, do not grieve. If you could see
what the land is doing! Towering fern-trees
thirty meters high, breaking the rocks
into soil. Not like the mosses you once knew.
If you could see it, you would not recognize
that rocky shore. You would rejoice.

No, we would not have recognized it.
Nor did we recognize this clouded water
downstream, full of loam and bacteria.
The effluvia of progress swirling round our own
thin roots, taking the air and the light.
From a glorious sunlit world
that did not know what it did.
Nor did it matter much in the end,
if it was death that had killed us, or life.

LEPIDODENDRON

Saint of the world's first forest,
giant of the Carboniferous trees,
your curled crown towered over mortals.

Soaking up and enriching the air,
you made a sky so pure
that everything grew into it, dragonflies
like hawks, millipedes like anacondas.
Everything stood taller
in your shade.

The mushrooms, the molds
built to break your body down
had not been born.
Nothing could rot you.
Incorruptible, your stately body
sank into the earth
and was compressed by the million feet
of the lives you nursed,
into the dark shine of anthracite,
and deeper, into diamond.

ARCHAEOTHYRIS

When I was a child, the jungle shriveled.
Once a lush wet greenness half the world wide,
it shrank and pulled away from itself,
into leaf-islands dotting the earth like mold.

I do not mind the dryness.
It suits me to scamper in crackling leaves,
to lay my leathery eggs in the damp
between roots of a moss-tree.
I am not given to weep as my cousins do;
my hide is tough
and my small hands clever. I survive.

Tell me, then, why when I lay my head down in my nest,
I see my ancestral seas spanning the world. Why I dream
of running in a rain that never ends,
swimming the endless flood of runoff
with my weak porous cousins who need water
to breathe. Who, in my dream, are alive.

DIMETRODON

You do not know them,
these newfangled body-shapes
tumbling out of the cereal box
with your own toy likeness.
They are not of your time.
When you sunned yourself in the desert heat
they were not even a thought:
as many million years from you
as apes from tyrannosaurs.

Their line diverged from yours
before you were born. If you had children
left alive today, they would be odd cousins
to the cats and the platypi:
knobbly, not-quite-yet-furred,
great scaleless gnawers of bones.

Long before the terrible lizards rose,
you had died. The world had burned again:
ten million volcanoes a blistering hole
in its side. You had choked on the ash.
You were bones. Dust.

You never sparred with a stegosaur,
ran from a raptor. Yet you have grown used
to careless baby apes parading them around
the kitchen table with you, as if these were your friends,
as if these were your enemies.
You have learned to play your role,
to growl and chase as reptiles do
on your lumbering scaleless legs.

Perhaps they are your new kin, after all–
at least the reptiles know what it is
to be remembered in toy form, carelessly,
kindly, a little bit wrong.

ADA HOFFMANN

2. THE AGE OF REPTILES

PROTEROSUCHUS

The world was burned, dead, and rotten,
again. The fabulous beasts
that you draw in your books,
horns and crests, plates and spines,
had not been born. These were the days
of swamp and desert, empty days.
Nothing much lived: nothing you
would call interesting.
Just teeth. Just hungry throats.
Just us.

Crouched in fetid waters
where even the fish choked and died,
we floated, waiting.
Weeks, sometimes. Our hearts
beat sluggish, cold,
a pallid system needing little,
for little was ours. We could wait months
before the hunger gnawed hard.
Months for just one
of the little beaked pigs
who, alone save us, had lived in any numbers:
for one little piggy to dip one toe
in our sulfurous pond.
Then:
Snap.
We swallowed.

We know why your books do not speak of us.
We are not long-necked exotics
or galloping nightmares.
Children would not swoon and squeal
at the sight of our lumbering forms:
they would say, "Oh,
an alligator."
These bodies of ours, cold and floating,

have never much needed to change.
Flame and frost, plague and famine
will not crack our spines. All we need
is water, time, a single prey species
to redden the sludge that we live in:
a single vein of stolen blood
to water the dead earth to life.

SCLERACTINIA

There was coral before. Do you remember?
Hard shells and slippery polyp fingers.
Between them, whole schools and shoals:
clownfish amid the weeds and seahorses
frolicking. A wide finned bounty.

That was before the oceans choked.
Coral is dead. Coral is ten million years gone.

I am not a coral. My little shell, my hungry arms, these
are not my inheritance. Coral did not leave them here
for a worthy heir. Coral is gone, and I am
coral's tiny fourth cousin,
anchored to the rock, eating the current.

They will call me a coral in years to come,
when my children's children climb
till islands rise from our bones.
And when the sea burns, when we are death-white
and broken, they will call me coral still.
I am not a coral. Coral is a home. I am one polyp,
reaching out for what the waves can give.

STAURIKOSAURUS

The scientists were so surprised
to find you in Brazil,
they named you after it:

as if the greatest monsters
should have roamed the northern heights which,
by coincidence, birthed the blond men
who studied them.

No, you were a jungle creature.
Bursting with purpose
as you dodged the bully crocodiles
who dwarfed you. Not for long,
their crawling reign.
You and your cousins,
quick and small and southern,
were about to rule the world.

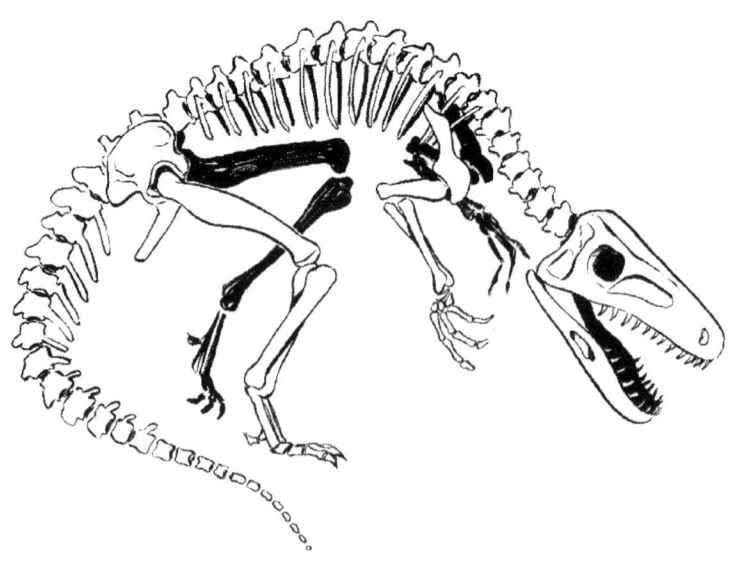

PROTOAVIS

You were knocked away by the water-wall,
you and ten small creatures
both like and unlike you.
Swept away and drowned when the river rose,
dashed to pieces under the sand.

A man found you, later,
all the half-crushed broken parts.
He jigsaw-toyed with them,
trying one fit, then another,

and what was this?
your skull, a limb, some vertebrae,
lumps that could be the anchor points
for feathers-
put together a certain way,
squinted at, seen wishfully,
you were the most amazing thing.

Look, said the man. *Look at this,
a true bird, millions of years
before we thought there were birds.*

The others scoffed.

You were not a bird. You ran and hopped,
and could not out-hop the flood.
But you had been jumbled
half-broken in the rock for so long,
a Rorschach blankness folding and re-folding.
When you are crushed you can be anything
you want to be.

PLATEOSAURUS

Long before we understood
the descent of species,
we knew you.
Your strange, huge limbs
lay trapped in the petrified mud.

Dragon, we called you.
Worm that walks, winglessly snaking
through the primordial swamp,
seething with venom (as you chewed
the placid leaves of ancient plants).
Cattle-eating, bellowing,
calling for sacrifice

until your weight pushed you
down in unglamorous mud,
sinking with the innocence
of the herbivore you were,
and left the incrimination
of the size of you
behind.

STEGOSAURUS
after Walt Disney's *Fantasia*

An empty head. A walnut-head.
A head, you say, of clouds and leaf-munching,
not a tactics-head.
It is not my head you look at
when you storm out of the woods,
at the climax of our little film,
teeth shining.

Whenever I look at you,
I see double. My head is entranced with
the music's arrhythmic thud,
the symbolism of all of this,
as, wiser, my hips turn to run.

This was preordained. A sacrifice.
This music that beats and throbs around us,
you know, is the music of sacrifice.
The spring ritual. The chosen one.
We must eat one another or die.
It is, you say, a love story.
For who does a monster love more than his prey?

You bite my neck,
but it is not my head you want,
this scrawny, walnut, brainless thing.
It is my hips you want, these round,
fat, mouthwatering hips, this feast
you can render to pieces and swallow.
But these hips and this tail carry spines-

Slashing down on your face.
Again. And again.

Your teeth loosen. Not enough:
you are inches from me every step of this dance.

My shoulders a garland of blood.
Give in, lovely walnut,
you croon. *I am compassionate;
why should you suffer? Death is better
than an empty walnut life, doing nothing
of consequence. Dead, this suffering
will end, and you will feed me.*

I know my place. I know this sacrifice.
I do not know why I back away. Why my foot
hits the water, and yet walks on.
My hips would know. Perhaps it is
a step in this dance-

I am shaking.
I am half in love with your teeth.
I am walking backwards, wading
in water now up to my chest.

But you, on the shore, open your jaws
in a wail. *Come back, you traitor.
What monster would leave me here,
leave me to starve?
Are you so wicked, so devoid
of compassion, that you do not care
what I need from you?*

I know your law. But it is my hips-
my round, strong, beautiful hips
full of muscle, hips that drive
lumbering life-bearing legs and strong feet:
my hips have always known where to go.
They carry me over the water,
through two-foot tripping silt and spray
where you cannot follow.

You gnash your teeth on the shoreline,
calling for the food
that no longer loves you.

BRONTOSAURUS
after *The Land Before Time*

Serious people do not speak this name.
Even when the papers came through-
despite what we thought, it seems you were
yourself all along-serious people
did not believe. There have been too many
mistakes. Always some reason
why the picture we had of you
was not quite right:
the missing head, of course. The tail,
not quite long enough. The feet, perhaps,
too little.

But we put you on our postage stamps.
We made you into toys.
Five years old and mudpie-handed,
we did not care if the skull on your spine
was yours: we cared
if you outran the predators
snapping through sedges,
if you made it to your valley.

Of course, there was no valley.
When the winds changed
and the continents bucked, as they always do,
you simply died. The sun beat down,
the rivers dried-

Or maybe not. Yours
was no age of cataclysms, no great burning.
Maybe what happened was gentle. Maybe
the swamps were thick and green.
The cycads grew tall. Juicy leaves
fell around you like snow and you simply
ran out of sequels
at a ripe old age.

ADA HOFFMANN

If you were never real,
then you can have your happy ending.

BLATTODEA

If you want to live forever,
be small. Flame and famine take
the biggest first. Be unremarkable.
Hide in a crevice, in the shadow
of a shadow, and never come out.

If you want to live forever, shrink.
Be leathery and flexible so as to fall
under elephantine feet and scurry off unscathed.
Learn to run. Hide. Hide again.

Empty yourself of original thought.
Make your mind small, no, smaller:
the body must live, scurry, eat, fuck, hide,
when even the braincase is torn from you.
You'll live in the bonecracking cold
and the withering sun without water.
Hold your breath, longer, longer, longer.
Eat nothing. Eat garbage. Eat the rotting bodies
of your friends. In lean months, eat
the meagre, sticky film behind a postage stamp.

You will still know the nudge
of a friend's feet-tips; a thousand friends.
You will still know the scent of a lover.
You will have children, fifty million children
and their children's children's children.
You will thrive. You will be everywhere.
And because you are everywhere,
fortunes will be spent on destroying you.
You will be poisoned, stomped on, drowned,
starved, stuck to boards, torn in two.
Your tormentors will tear their hair and scream:
Why won't it die?

You will smell like rot because you have lived there;
like illness because you have lived there too;
like hate because big creatures,
fragile in their frills and claws, do not trust
what they cannot destroy.
Little will be left of you.
And is that what you want?

ARCHAEOPTERYX

Settled and nested in what, to you,
was the present, you never imagined
the quick-flit jewel-bodies of hummingbirds,
the falcon's deadly plunge, the ostrich,
the quizzical flamingo. To you,
you were the pinnacle of all
small-bodied quick-snapping things:
the air your palace. A song your home.

Or did you dream, at your perch,
of the thunderous terror birds of the Andes?
Did you preen at your own little black-bristled tail,
remembering the brilliant eyes
of yet-to-be-born peacocks, and despair?

Perhaps you felt all your life
like only half a thing, and strained
in a direction only half-real,
ashamed that you could not mold yourself,
by force of will, into all
that could ever be made of you.

MAGNOLIA

Come to me, my symbiote,
my love: look what I have made.
A white and violet petal,
delicate as the rain,
unfolding for you.

Come to me, my symbiote,
my love, and taste my nectar.
Sticky-sweet fuel
for your quick-buzzing wings,
for I love your constant flit
from place to place,
away from my green repose
and back again.

Come to me, cover yourself
in my golden breath
so that seeds will grow far from here
and children I will never see
may raise their white-violet heads.

In this same way,
your own hidden nest,
chewn paper thick with buzzing sisters
and daughters and aunts,
will fill to bursting.

Come to me, my symbiote,
my love, and admire yourself.
How different we are, you and I.
Yet if you had not shaped yourself
to please me, and I you,
the earth would not have burst into bloom.

IGUANADON

No one had heard the word *dinosaur*
when they pulled your teeth from the stone.
Gentlemen in tailcoats examined your fragments.
Debated:
what animal had teeth like these?
A rhinoceros? No. An iguana. But larger
than any iguana on earth.

These were modern scientific men,
not like the ancients who would have called you
a monster, a dragon, a god. There was only
one God, and this God--said the strongest of them--
had not made you a lizard. You were no iguana:
you were an elephantlike thing all your own.
No creature like you
could evolve from mere lizards.
You were proof of creation *ex nihilo*.

This while they worked at you from scraps,
puzzling over a thighbone, a knee-joint,
a thumb. Placing the bones this way and that,
revising their own earnest creation
from the almost
nothing left of the past.

ADA HOFFMANN

HADROSAURUS

By the rushing river in the blooming spring,
you called for your lover. You were not yet complete.
Not the love-helmets, head-trumpets,
unicorn horns of your descendants.
But you possessed the heart for it,
the need. The song that you played
in the cavities of your skull.
Come to me. Love me. Want me. Please.

You were singing when they dug you out
from the marl pit. When Cope and Marsh descended
on the room where your polished skull shone.

They were fast friends then. Cope with his moustache
and his gentleman's swagger. Marsh, gruff and frowning
through his brush of a beard. In Berlin,
they had bonded over beer and a love
of the ancient. They'd named species for each other.

Cope, who owned the pits, glowed with pride
for you, his beautiful lizard, his precious
skull. Marsh's eyes darted this way, that.
Taking down all of it, desperately searching
for flaws. As if a flaw would justify
what was in his mind--when there was
no justification but your time-echoed song.
Want me. Please. Want me-

The song Marsh heard in his bones
while he spoke to the foreman, secretly, after.
Pressed a fist of bills into his palm.
You don't understand. Cope is unworthy.
He has made errors. Please-
send the next one to me.

Cope would never forgive him.
Hence the war, the bones dynamited,
the robbers, the bribes -
for fifteen years,
until it ruined them both.

You did not know you were the golden apple
setting alliances ablaze.
You in your honest unelaborate song.
Come to me. Love me.
You pined, through the ages,
for a warm-scaled mate:
but it was us who fought to have you.

ADA HOFFMANN

OVIRAPTOR

Stop.
Thief.

I do not know what I took.
I was guarding the nest when the storms came–
guarding you--and then the choking dust,
the ash, the grave. Then these bone-plaster men,
waking me out of my sleep, accusing.

This species does not brood its nest.
How could it? Cold-blooded, primitive,
soulless. She stole them.

I raise my hackles and open my mouth,
but their hands already stroke my brow,
soothing. Mock-soft. *We understand.*
You are hungry, not wicked; what could be wrong
with hunger?

And I was hungry when I laid you.
Hungry as any mother, staying at the nest,
giving up the hunt to keep you warm.

They measure my rotted-out eyeholes,
my scraped-clean skull. They explain me.
Did you know? My beak, my strong smooth jaw,
is shaped to crack you open and devour you.
My swift legs, to run with you,
far from the punishing horns
of your real mother.

It is all right, they assure me.
it is what you had to do. Any woman would eat a child
if she had to, if it was this or starvation.

I do not know. Can I trust my memory?
I think you were mine. I think I loved you.
But these voices ring so loud, so sure, so vivid
that I can see it in my mind. I can feel
your shell crack, your yolk drip down my chin.
Perhaps I am wrong. Maybe I ate you, after all,

my egg, my tiny everything,
who I covered with my body
when the storms came.

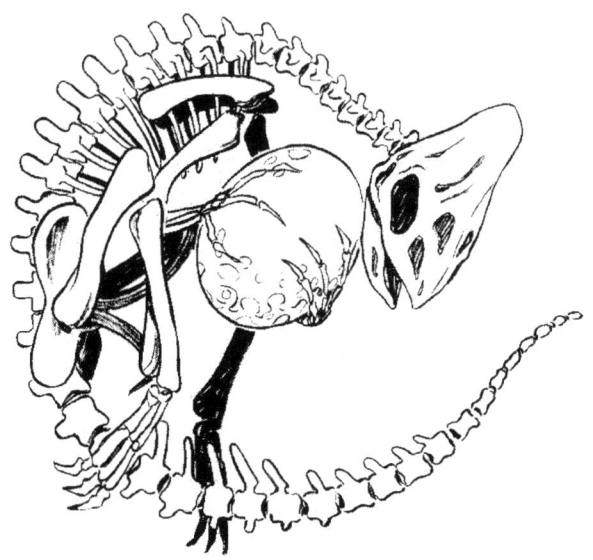

EDMONTONIA

You preach against an excess
of armor, the spikes at our shoulders,
the hardened carapace dragged along
lest fangs or grit get through.
Of course this is foreign to you,
the soft-furred ones, who groom and purr
and forgive. You want to understand us.
You want us to roll on our bellies,
defenseless -

          (- in a world
of soft grasses, an imaginary
haven of murmurs and lightest
caresses -)

                - you see thickness
as guilt, as giving up.

But watch as we spar on the shores.
Hear the bellow of victory, the rough
thumping roll down rocky slopes. Watch us burst
and shrug through the underthorns
of the thickening woods. Watch the clash
which is joy because we may clash and clash
again, the bold heavy beat
of a heart that knows weight and grins
in its midst. You who can taste
each other's skin, you do not know
the intimacy of shared armor, shared sharpness,
shared strength.

BACTROSAURUS

We dusted away the rock to find
your ancient bones, and the curled tumor
eating at them.

Without radiation or medicine,
you had died in pain.

We expected nothing less: we knew
that our ailments, like us,
had evolved. We only wondered,
as we pulled the white sheet over your skull,
how long it had been since our bodies
learned to eat themselves.

VELOCIRAPTOR
after *Jurassic Park*

Run.
Run.

You should have been a chicken. Tiny and cheeping,
eagle wings aflap atop your prey. You should have punctured
little reptile-sheep with those toe-claws, gnawed at their necks
while you dragged the bodies back to your nest.
That was where it should have ended. But we-

We needed more teeth.

We wanted to run for our lives. Our real lives.
Real like ragged breath and the pumping of legs.
To fall at last into safety,
the armoured car, the lover's arms.
To huddle, spent, shaking, to slow the hammer heart
which shouts to our ribs, again and again,
that this is enough, that we won, that we lived.

Forgive us: we made you our monsters.
Or do not forgive: that's the point, isn't it?
Spill our intestines. Drag our flailing bodies through the grass.
Break our windows. Throw open our doors. Hunt us.
Hunt us-
    and let
        the worthy
            live.

THERIZINOSAURUS

Descendant of sword-toothed predators, you
had sworn off meat. You were proud of it,
flaunting the outsized grabber claws
that you reserved for pulling weeds
from the seabed. You lay down,
belly-up, explaining your gentleness.
You could not understand
why anyone preferred savage carnivores
to yourself.

These claws, you said, were not for rending but
for clinging to a lover. They might terror-squirm,
unable to move for your weight. But you did not
hunt them. Not so much as broke their skin.
You never understood
why, as soon as you carelessly
allowed it, each one ran.
Surely, if your teeth did not enter their flesh
and their blood did not fill you,
you could never have hurt them at all.

QUETZALCOATLUS

Serpent of the sky, furred serpent,
shadow-wing sailing the wind.
Borne on the breeze you swing swift,
your beak a twinned spear,
scatter a scared burst of feathers
on the yawning steppes.

CAPITALSAURUS

All that was left of you was one bone
in the hands of a soil-smudged sewer-man
between First and F Streets.
One bone--a shard from a spine.
And what could you have been? How big?
How fearsome? We charted out
your teeth, your skull, your tail.

We named you after us: you were the only monster
here before us. We delighted in having a thing to name.
At the peak of the drama, someone gathered
a score of schoolchildren, clutching pencils
and notepaper, their drawings of scissor-mouthed
glorious beasts. They whispered and poked
as they watched. It was for future generations,
we said, that we named you Official District Dinosaur.
For who could bear the name of this place but

a lumbering meat-eater,
hungry and cruel, and so big,
about whom we know nothing.

We always want the found dead,
the martyrs, the murdered,
to be ours--or what good are they?

Ask the hundred Nacotchtank women
rotting to the bone below the Potomac.
Femurs, scapulae, hip bones and skulls:
ask if *their* bones ever lit the eyes
of a class of eager eight-year-olds.
Not enough sharp teeth to make them Official Anything
for the gun-germ-steel men who moved in atop them.
(We assume you had teeth, and a tail,
attached to that shard of spine somewhere.)

You know. They tell you their secrets:
they ride on your broken back through the ghost-woods.
Beast and tribe together, you share
the silent irony of dead things.
Hands to the gap, where that one vertebra
fell in the mud, they guide you
across grave-rivers, under black skies.
Why should you care about towers and presidents,
or the men who call your name
without knowing who you were?
You snap at a wheeling ghost-bird, and move on.

TYRANNOSAURUS

I am six. I am looking at your teeth.
I am calculating the volume
of your excavator jaw.

They have stripped you, chipped the stone
from your naked frame, unsheathed you
from feathers or scales. Leaving this skull
with holes I could put my hand through.
Unshielded from the wind and the din
of this crane-necked crowded room.

I am thinking of being inside you.
Plucked from the ground with serrated tongs
and swallowed. I am not thinking of pain.
Pressure, yes. The loss of breath,
the darkness and heat of you.
I would die of fear. But your jaws
are round and strong and I am small
and I want to crawl inside.

I will be old and never realize
why I crave an armor made of razor bones.
Why I am hungry for men with teeth.
Only a tyrant, the fiercest of monsters,
could ever contain me.

ADA HOFFMANN

OSMUNDA

Ask the cartomancer what your future holds.
Watch her slowly spread her hands, aghast.
This time it takes only a moment's blast
      to scatter, shatter, slam
          your reptile world away.

And what will you do, little one,
      when the bones of your lovers
        lie white on the clay?

Wrap yourself around a sharpened rib.
Press the point to the centre
of your palm. Weep, until it occurs to you
that reptiles do not cry,
nor do the dead.

Nor do the mushrooms and ferns
which have sprouted, sucking
at what rots when left behind.
The dew on fractal tendril-leaves
which open to the slowly lighting sky;
nor was death ever so green.

3. THE AGE OF MAMMALS

PTILODUS

And when the dust had gone to dust,
when the fires died and ferns struggled up
from the ashes, I found you.
Soft-tailed smallness like mine,
counting acorns in the hollow of a tree, as if
it was not, after all, the end.

We did not know that we had inherited
this world, the hot dry dead plains
and skeletal forests--we knew
only that all was death,
yet we breathed.

You wrapped me in your tail and fussed over
the fur of my head. I, skittish,
shivering--I who had known only
reptile lovers, long cold teeth
in the guts of the night. I had not known
that I could love gentleness. That a warm,
safe den, worn round with flowers and leaves,
could hold me. Hesitant,
I nuzzled in your fur
and traced your scars.

You'll leave, you chittered.
Everyone leaves. You had seen your family,
all your siblings, torn apart
by the last of the taloned giants.
I did not argue. I had run
from tree to tree, den to den,
never stopping since the flames began,
as if a small soft thing could outrun time.
Mountainous skulls littered the ground,
back then, and nothing lived long.

Yet in your arms, under the warm leaves,
the panicked knot of me, by an inch,
unclenched.

You were the one who ran.
Finding at last the little dew-claw
of my thumb, retracted, under fur.
You had seen claws like this before,
ten times this size, claws in the throats
of your children. You turned and fled,
out of the tree, out of sight,
bristled like a frightened spear of fur
across the dead plains.

Where you had trod, even the ferns
raised their heads higher.

PLESIADAPIS

There is a missing chapter here.
So the man of science thinks,
squinting at the fossils
and scratching his nose.

This tree-dweller, tarsier-like,
chittering--at first you were so small.
Somehow you grew. Somehow you became
the most intelligent, the strongest,
the fittest to rule. Somehow in between
that burned-out ferny beginning
and the rising of the pyramids,
you became us.

There must be some royal birthmark.
Maybe the thumb-claws,
lightly opposed.
Maybe in your still-small,
growing, brain.

Life rewards the fittest, after all.
You cannot simply have been
a lucky squirrel.

Did you feel lucky in life?
Did you feel like a father of kings?

Tell us, where in our lineage
is the turning point: the first monkey
or ape, or little bushy-tailed thing,
who was large enough to look at the world
and think,
    mine?

AZOLLA

Green, we said to each other. Grow.
Until our green fronds spanned the ocean.
It was warm then, and the sun seared down
on mirror waves and weedy shade.
Fish and crabs, anemones, stars
thronged up and down in our borders.
Feasting on sea-ferns. Warmed by the sky.

Surely ours was an empire greater
than any at sea. We were there to give life.
We did not know that, when we fell,
some warmth went with each of us.

There were more of us than any thousand fish
could ever eat. All we wanted was to grow.
But when we were done, stems frosted,
waves gone still and white in the world's winter,
the sea had grown smaller,
and the green had gone.

ADA HOFFMANN

BASILOSAURUS

"Progress," said your brothers. Further up
across the mountains, but you could not tear your eyes
from your ancestral nursery. The sea,
deep, dark, clear.

Push off from the shore. Float in the waters.
Watch the light that shades from ripple-blue
to black. Snap your jaws, every once in a while,
for a little fish.

These fish might know something you don't,
fat and shining as they are, crowding the bright dark world
your brothers fled. There was never any need to leave.
There were always multitudes, here and above,
vibrant with deepwater's song.

BALUCHITHERIUM

A statue of you, life-size,
straddles this forest path.
We are meant to walk underneath,
my mother and brother and my small self,
calmly following under your belly.
I do not have to duck.

I am at the age of
wanting to walk under everything.
Wanting to measure myself.
Why isn't everything fitted to me?
My size, or the size
of my outstretched arms,
or large enough to swallow me,
or large like a room.
I want to live under a breathing animal
and always look up.

I want to look out my bedroom window
and watch massive beasts on promenade.
I want to see the earth as it was,
or as I imagine it was:
a peaceful congregation of giants.
It has not yet occurred to me,
in my childhood, that I am the giant.
That I, now, am all that is left.

MEGALODON

We have nothing of you but your teeth-
but what teeth!
Teeth like the tongues of dragons,
longer than a kitchen knife,
forked and serrated. So many rows
of these teeth. A man could walk
at full height through your jaw.

You must have been a terror,
bigger than dinosaurs,
bulldozing the ocean.
Those big teeth shredded whales,
yet of the bulwark of you
in which those teeth were planted,
we have nothing. Strange that a monster
like you could be built so softly.
You needed only death, and the gentlest
of currents, to wear away to nothing.

HIPPARION

I was small, and not yet hooved.
A modest creature. But I knew
the wind in my mane, and the sun-warmed
soil beneath my toes.

When I found my way out of my small steppe,
the hills pooled out every which way,
studded with flowers' heads,
bobbing with green.

The world opened up before me.
And I ran.

And I ran.

PHORUSRHACOS

You had not died. Your teeth had receded
to a smooth, sharp beak. A hook at the tip
to tear your prey. Feathered arms,
a fluttering vestige of wings.
You yourself stomped your talons,
stalked the plains. Your call was a scream:
burrowing ground-squirrels hid their heads.
You swallowed rabbits whole. Your songbird sisters
lit on the branches before you, chirped greeting.
Everything had changed its shape, even the pushed-high land
you stood on, even you. But the heart within you,
once the heart of a reptile--that heart beat.
You raised a voice once almost silenced,
now strong. You called for your prey.

SMILODON

The young apes under the trees,
gnawing on nuts, berries, and old bones,
fireless, knifeless--the apes
watch the dark for your shadow.

The sinuous leap of you, the spotted flash,
the muscular jaw closing to pierce the carotid.

It's so fast. Blink,
and the tiger will have you.

The young apes take turns
keeping watch in the moonlight.
One of them picks up a sharp stick,
files it down on an outcropped rock,
stabs it into the earth.

If only we could be as quick and strong
as the long teeth that come in the night.
We would eat our fill. We would rest,
languid and warm as a cat in the sunlight,
pillowed on bellies of blood.

ADA HOFFMANN

HOMO HABILIS

The steaming hippopotamus,
sprawled on the fossilized riverbed,
was dead. You had not killed it.
You only had the idea,
that most daring of thoughts.

Small as you were, you knew
how to chip off the edges of stone
to butcher small dead things
that you found amid the leaves.

Fearfully, one of you crept up
and tested your blade on its hide.
Dead. It easily split;
the meat tasted fresh.

The whole hippopotamus, when found,
was scraped raw. Bones cracked.
Tendons cut. You had not killed it.

The vultures and hyenas did not dare
dispute your claim, at first.
The herds, the dire elk,
the rhinocerids and mammoth,
milled on, undisturbed.

You hefted your stone in your hand
and considered them.

MEGATHERIUM

They shouted, the humans.
Move faster. Were they shouting at me?
Perhaps at each other,
the spindly monkeyforms with the spear-throwers.
Perhaps to hurry,
before I thought to hit them
with these tree-shredding claws.

Bald monkeys were no threat to me.
I am large and my hide is thick.
I contemplated them. Forest creatures
will scurry, rushing this way and that.
But what would they accomplish?
I did not see a tiger here
to run from, or a rabbit
to hunt.

Were they hunting me?
Yet those spears, even thrown, were no danger,
so long as they did not get close.
My claws were the size of their faces.
Why would they get close?

It was certainly a mystery,
these humans with their little tools.
I thought about it until the spears struck
and thought fled.

ADA HOFFMANN

URSUS

Consider the cave bear, stretched here
as though there was life in that skin,
fangs still bared, pebble-eyes gleaming.
Consider these flowers and herbs
we strew before it. The Great Bear,
strongest of beasts, our saviour.

The bear is born small.
We all are. A round ball, enticing
to tigers and wolves — and, worse,
to its father. Consider the male bear,
a berry-fed beast, who will tear a mother's cubs
to pieces and take her by force.
Consider the mother bear, famous with rage
because she has to be. Step between her
and the children, and you are that tearing claw,
that grinning tooth, the thing that must be destroyed.
If she is vigilant, if she crushes everything
in her path, it is possible
her children will live out the year.

As she did.

Consider the cubs, most of all.
Close your eyes and breathe these herbs:
remember that part of you, small and squalling,
who knows what it is to run.
To be small. Other beasts are smaller
even than the cub; other beasts are prey
their whole lives, but that does not matter so much
to a child whose world is fangs and blood.
Flattening itself at the back of the den
while a man growls at the door.

Until the child is grown, and he becomes what he fears.
Until the child is grown, and she becomes

a guardian, heedless of all but cornered rage.
He says:
I am not above the way of beasts. Stop cowering.
We all become large, and I am large now,
and will take my turn at what is mine.
She says:
Never again. Not me. You will not take this.
If I must destroy you and everything else,
so be it. I will do it. You will fail.
We all become large, and I am large now.
Both hearing a grown man's growl in the back of their mind,
still, that dark cold press.

Know this, child, as you bow before
the bear. We are none of us free.
You can grow to be strong. You can scheme.
You can kill. It will not stop the thing you fear.

We made a good try at it, didn't we?
Consider the bear, grown man,
from your glass-steel tower, from your smoke-choked
factory floor, from your drone.
Was it ever enough? We have killed the world
(again), flattened the forests,
burned the deserts, salted the sea.
Their bodies lie before you, humans too,
a starved continent of limbs. And the earth
below you, poisoned and shaking,
softly smiles. She knows this cycle;
she has seen it before.

We are so large now, so strong.
But we have never forgotten our monsters.

EPILOGUE: MEMENTO MORI

we look at the stars
we look at the stars

One day I woke up and the hands at the throat of the earth
were my own. One day I woke up
and the world was a child whom I could not save.
One day I woke up and I saw all the monsters
within me: the molluscs hiding
afraid in their shells, the snarling tyrannosaurs,
the giggling apes who confused their fear
with cleverness, and I no longer made any excuse.

So I walked out into the garden
and buried my face in the loamy green.

These flowers will die. The wide leafy springlands
will die. The rabbits will die. The long old trees,
the elephants, the whale-songs will die
at my hand. Though I never meant to.

But if it takes a million years to bloom again, still,
life knows the likes of us. Life knows how to hide
in the rocks, the swamps, to be small
and rebuild.

For a while, anyway. For the time we are allotted
until the sun swells up to meet us
in swallowing flame

    we look at the stars

until the universe spins out exhausted,
into dust, into cold

    we look at the stars

Every beast on this earth is a murderer.
But one day we woke up and could look at our hands:
we were beginning to understand the blood,
what it cost, how it got there. And there was still
a fraction of a second before dusk.

Who will come after us? After the bombs,
the floods, the meteors, the simple march
of generations. One day, a mind will look back
which is not our own
and cannot fathom us

much as we, in the end, could fathom nothing
but our human fear. All the world's previous lives
watch with their skull-socket eyes from the rock,
which has swallowed any wisdom
they might once have spoken. We read, in those teeth,
what we wish to.

Yet there is time. Even now, in this single fly-flicker life.
The grass and the flowers still live. And we know
what they need from us, here and now, before the fires
which will swallow us too. In the face
of hunger and death and the forever-falling stars,
grass grows, grass which springs up new
from the flame. Grass which will outlive us.
The grass that I rolled in, that morning.

Then I rose. Dried my tears. Baked bread. Ate fruit.
Wrapped my arms around my lover.
Dug into the dirt with my hands and let the stardust,

eaten and shat by a million billion lives,
fall through my fingers.

When they pry my bones from the rock,
they will not know if I was good or bad,
wise or foolish, only that I lived,
and they will make of that what they will.

ACKNOWLEDGMENTS

This project began in 2014 with a single poem, "Tyrannosaurus." I had no idea where it would go from there, but I already knew it would be a series. Most of the poems were written between 2015 and 2017, and the remaining time was spent dithering, procrastinating, fiddling with individual lines, and figuring out where and how I wanted to publish them.

I owe thanks to the editors at Asimov's, Liminality, Mythic Delirium, Strange Horizons, and Uncanny, who took chances on some of the early individual poems before the full project had taken a stable shape.

Salie Snapdragon was a valued collaborator in the later portions of the writing process, enthusiastically suggesting creatures to write about, helping with research, and providing other assistance. AJ Odasso, Maigen Turner, Izzy Wasserstein, Merc Fenn Wolfmoor, and others whose names have been lost provided valuable beta reading help at all stages. In particular they talked me out of including a bunch of intrusive, explanatory epigraphs with each poem, which would have been a terrible idea. Kelsey Liggett, my illustrator and cover designer, was a joy to work with and well worth the money.

My agent, Hannah Bowman, was not heavily involved in this book, but she is a wonderful agent. She helped me to talk through my plans and make sure they wouldn't conflict with contracted projects or with future novel sales. Dr. Guy Narbonne, from whom I took a paleontology course once, and both of my parents, who cheerfully fed my special interest in dinosaurs as a child, are also owed thanks. All paleontological errors in this book are mine alone, and not Dr. Narbonne's fault.

Several poems, including "Stegosaurus," "Therizinosaurus," and "Ptilodus," were inspired by experiences with specific people; these shall remain nameless.

Finally, thanks go to Paul Church, Jacqueline Flay, Dave Fredsberg, RB Lemberg, Aelin Shadowpine, Brett Tucker, and my "friends at the pub" for the continual friendship and support that have made it possible for me to continue with projects like these. Thank you all.

ABOUT THE AUTHOR

Ada Hoffmann is the author of the space opera novel THE OUTSIDE, the collection MONSTERS IN MY MIND, and dozens of speculative short stories and poems. Ada's work has been a finalist for the Philip K. Dick Award (2020, THE OUTSIDE), the Compton Crook Award (2020, THE OUTSIDE), and the WSFA Small Press Award (2020, "Fairest of All"). She is the winner of the Friends of the Merrill Collection Short Story Contest (2013, "The Mother of All Squid Builds a Library") and a two-time Rhysling award nominee (2014 for "The Siren of Mayberry Crescent" and 2017 for "The Giantess's Dream").

Ada was diagnosed with Asperger syndrome at the age of 13, and is passionate about autistic self-advocacy. Her Autistic Book Party review series is devoted to in-depth discussions of autism representation in speculative fiction. Much of her own work also features autistic characters.

Ada is an adjunct professor of computer science at a major Canadian university, and she did her PhD thesis (in 2018) on teaching computers to write poetry. Under her legal name, she has published eight papers and presented her work at conferences around the world. She is a former semi-professional soprano, tabletop gaming enthusiast, and LARPer. She lives in eastern Ontario with a curious black cat.

Made in the USA
Middletown, DE
21 August 2021